SURREY STEAM

Scenes from the

MICHAEL WELCH

Capital Transport

CONTENTS

Front cover The North Downs, on the horizon, provide the perfect backdrop to this splendid view of Maunsell N Class 'Mogul' No.31852 at Betchworth with the 4.04pm Redhill to Reading train. This photograph was taken on a lovely spring day in May 1963. Note the level crossing, which carries a secondary road across the railway, and the station house at the far end of the westbound platform. The latter housed a signal frame, worked by a porter–signalman, which was installed in 1934 as a replacement for a separate signal box adjacent to the level crossing. Originally, there were two signal boxes at this small intermediate station! The siding in the foreground gave access to the Dorking Greystone Lime Company's quarry, which continued to generate rail traffic until about 1960. Note the tiny goods yard, on the right, with its heaps of coal awaiting delivery by local merchants. The yard was still open for railborne traffic at the time of this picture, but closed in September 1964. *Roy Hobbs*

Back cover The quadruple track Waterloo to Bournemouth line ran through Surrey for a relatively short distance, only about twenty miles, but is probably the route best remembered by steam enthusiasts if only because it was the last in the county to retain regular steam working. In fact, the line could justly claim to be Great Britain's last steam-worked express passenger route. In this classic shot, taken on 14th March 1965, Bulleid Pacific No.34090 *Sir Eustace Missenden Southern Railway* has just passed Weybridge station, which is discernible in the distance, at the head of a down express. The headcode discs indicate a Waterloo to Southampton Docks boat train. The line to Addlestone can be seen above the locomotive. *David Wigley*

Overleaf The 4.40pm London Bridge to Brighton via Oxted train is seen near Upper Warlingham, with 'Schools' Class 4–4–0 No.30901 *Winchester* in charge, on the glorious autumn evening of 2nd October 1961. This class was barred from the Uckfield line until about mid-1956, so consequently made few appearances in the Oxted area until the ban was lifted. A small contingent of the class was based at Brighton after their displacement from the bulk of their South Eastern Section duties. The 'Schools' Class engines were regularly rostered for the 7.17am Brighton to London Bridge and 4.40pm return working for a time, but they developed a habit of stalling on the bank out of Lewes, and were replaced on these trains by Bulleid Pacifics in early 1962. *Paul Leavens*

First Published 2001

ISBN 185414 238 0

Published by Capital Transport Publishing,
38 Long Elmes, Harrow Weald, Middlesex

Printed by CS Graphics, Singapore

INTRODUCTION

There is a commonly held misconception that Surrey is a county inhabited almost entirely by wealthy City stockbrokers and this impression probably dominates an outsider's view of the county. In contrast, the neighbouring counties of 'Kent, the Garden of England', and 'Sussex by the Sea' have a much kinder and appealing image, while Hampshire was, of course, associated with the late John Arlott and the relaxing game of cricket on the village green. Admittedly, Surrey probably numbers many stockbrokers among its population and its close proximity to London ensures its continuing prosperity, but this is an unfair perception because Surrey is certainly one of the prettiest, arguably *the* prettiest, of the Home Counties, a fact which is often overlooked; anyone who has walked in the Surrey Hills around Dorking would certainly testify to its particularly appealing landscape.

Railways came to the county as early as 1803 when the Surrey Iron Railway opened from Wandsworth to Croydon and later extended to Merstham. Ironically for a county which later became famous for its heavy passenger carryings, this line was built solely to move goods traffic. Development of the main line system commenced in the late 1830s when the London & Southampton and London & Croydon companies opened their routes from the Capital to Woking and Croydon respectively.

Surrey's railway system continued to grow during the remainder of the nineteenth century and, remarkably, even as late as the 1930s the suburban electric network was still expanding in order to cater for housing development on the edge of the Capital. Despite the dominance of electric passenger trains on many lines, steam traction continued to play a substantial role in many parts of the county moving freight and van trains and, of course, some lines remained solely steam-worked until the 1960s.

Despite its modest size and widespread electrification, Surrey offered enthusiasts a reasonable variety of steam-worked lines and perhaps the best remembered are, inevitably, the Waterloo to Bournemouth line, which runs through the county for some distance, and the attractive cross-country Reading to Redhill route which is close to the North Downs for much of its length. The former route was, of course, the last in the county to retain steam traction on regular scheduled services, though other lines did see occasional workings in connection with engineering operations or enthusiasts' specials right to the end of steam. Surrey was hardly a happy hunting ground for aficionados of the traditional steam-worked country branch line, because so many of the branches had long since been swallowed up by suburban housing development and electrified. The only exception was the Guildford to Horsham line which had a delightful rural atmosphere but did not serve any towns of importance, apart from Cranleigh. This line was the only one in Surrey to succumb to the late Doctor Beeching's infamous axe in the 1960s so, incredibly, Surrey retains its unique position as the only county to keep almost all of its original mileage intact. Apart from journeys through the county on railtours, one of which was the final train along the lovely Guildford to Horsham line, most of my memories revolve around numerous trips on the Bournemouth Line towards the end of steam. Many of these runs were behind Bulleid Pacifics and BR Standard Class 5MTs, some of which, to be candid, were in such poor mechanical condition it was tantamount to a national disgrace. Their parlous state was a result of the deliberate policy of maintaining the steam fleet at minimum cost until it was replaced by electric traction in July 1967. It was especially sad to see once-proud Bulleid Pacifics, which were such fine locomotives capable of sustained high-speed running, in service in such appallingly neglected condition, frequently minus name and numberplates.

I would like to record my appreciation to the many photographers who have made their irreplaceable slides available for publication. Without their kind assistance publication of this album would not have been possible. In addition, Terence Barry, David J. Fakes, Mike Hudson and Graham Mallinson have greatly assisted by reading the manuscript and suggesting many corrections and improvements. Finally, throughout the compilation of this album I have referred repeatedly to Alan A. Jackson's book *The Railway in Surrey* (Atlantic Transport Publishers), which I would unreservedly recommend to anyone interested in the history and development of railways in the county.

Burgess Hill, January 2001   Michael Welch

ASCOT TO VIRGINIA WATER

The Longmoor Military Railway's (LMR) 'Austerity' 2–10–0 No.600 *Gordon* makes a fine sight as it passes Sunningdale in the afternoon sunshine on 30th April 1966. No.600 was powering the return leg of a Railway Correspondence & Travel Society railtour which started at Waterloo and visited the LMR, before returning to London via Bentley, Ascot, Staines and Windsor. *Gordon* worked the train from Longmoor to Staines, where it gave way to BR Standard Class 5MT No.73114 *Etarre*. No.600 was built by the North British Locomotive Company in Glasgow in December 1943 and throughout its life was used solely for instructional purposes at the LMR. Unlike its sister engines it never ventured overseas. The line through Sunningdale was proposed by the Staines, Wokingham & Woking Junction Railway, which was incorporated in 1853 to build a line from Staines to the South Eastern Railway's Redhill to Reading line at Wokingham. It was worked from the outset by the LSWR, which acquired the line in 1878. *Neville Simms*

Photographed against an attractive background of autumn colours, Maunsell S15 4–6–0 No.30837 approaches Longcross Halt, between Virginia Water and Sunningdale, with a westbound freight on 24th October 1964. No.30837 survived to become the last active member of its class in BR service, and achieved fame when it worked two railtours to commemorate the S15 class in January 1966. Sadly these exploits did not ensure its survival and it subsequently fell victim to the scrapman's torch, though other examples of the class are preserved. Longcross Halt was opened in 1940 principally for the use of military personnel travelling to and from a base at Chobham Common. It was made available to the general public from 21st September 1942. The halt had no road access and offered only rudimentary shelters made of breeze blocks and corrugated iron. At the time of writing it is still open for passengers. *David Wigley*

WEYBRIDGE TO VIRGINIA WATER

Despite running bunker-first, the elegant design of Adams Class 0415 'Radial' No.30582 is still very much apparent in this shot taken near Addlestone on 19th March 1961. The locomotive was working a railtour organised by the Railway Enthusiasts Club that commenced at Waterloo and travelled from there to Guildford using a circuitous route via Windsor, Staines and Woking. The return journey was made through Leatherhead and Epsom. No.30582 was one of 71 engines designed by William Adams, and introduced in 1882 for LSWR suburban passenger services, this particular locomotive being constructed by Robert Stephenson & Co. in 1885. The start of electrification of the suburban trains in 1915 sounded the death knell for the majority of the class and withdrawals commenced in 1916. By the end of the 1920s No.30582 was one of only two survivors (another engine survived in private use in Kent) remaining in traffic on the Southern Railway, by this time employed on the Lyme Regis branch in the West Country, where it remained until withdrawn from service in July 1961. The Weybridge to Virginia Water line was opened in two stages, the first section to Chertsey opening on 14th February 1848. Financial difficulties delayed the final link on to Virginia Water for nearly twenty years, this eventually opening on 1st October 1866. *Paul Leavens*

A crowd of admirers gather around Adams 'Radial' No.30582 as it takes water at Chertsey during the course of working the railtour depicted in the previous photograph. Note the colourful pre-grouping non-corridor coaches forming the train. For some years Chertsey was, as previously mentioned, the terminus of a branch from Weybridge, but when authorisation was obtained for the extension to Virginia Water in 1864 an entirely new station was built on a different site. Reputed to be a twin of Netley station in Hampshire, a substantial two-storey Italianate villa was built, with a hipped and slated roof and delicately carved eaves brackets. A goods shed, cattle pens and sidings occupied the site of the original terminus and, amazing though it may seem, there was even a two-road locomotive shed at Chertsey, which lasted until 1937. *Graham Hoare*

Urie-designed S15 Class 4–6–0 No.30501 negotiates the tightly curving up Weybridge line platform at Virginia Water station with an eastbound freight, which was presumably destined for Feltham marshalling yard. This picture was taken on 23rd June 1957. The platform layout at Virginia Water followed the 'vee' of the converging lines, the station house being located on the up Wokingham line platform. *Trevor Owen*

L&SWR MAIN LINE

On 18th October 1964 the 'Midhurst Belle' railtour was run from Waterloo to mark the complete closure (beyond Petworth) of the Midhurst branch in West Sussex. The first stage of the journey used a roundabout route from Waterloo to Woking via Ascot and Bagshot, which involved traversing the Frimley Junction to Sturt Lane East Junction curve. This little known link, which connected the Aldershot to Ascot secondary route with the main Waterloo to Bournemouth line, was located about a mile east of Farnborough station and was electrified in 1939 for peak-hour Woking to Ascot services via Frimley. By 1964 these workings had long since ceased and the curve was earmarked for closure, so it is likely that this train was one of the last to use the connection. The third rail was confined to the local lines west of Pirbright Junction (on the main line) and Sturt Lane East Junction was the limit of electric workings along the main line at that time, although the third rail continued towards Farnborough for a few hundred yards in order to allow for over-runs. Here, Maunsell S15 4–6–0 No.30839 is depicted coming off the curve at Sturt Lane East *en route* to Woking, where a USA Class tank locomotive took over for the next stage of the journey. *David Wigley*

In this splendid action shot, Urie-designed 'King Arthur' 4–6–0 No.30748 *Vivien* heads westwards with an evening train between Brookwood and Farnborough on 27th June 1957. The train has just passed beneath an aqueduct which carries the Basingstoke Canal over the line. When the Bournemouth Line was widened at the turn of the century, two new tunnels were built using the cut-and-cover method and this entailed stopping up the canal while the work proceeded. The canal was reopened for traffic on 1st December 1902. No.30748, one of a batch of twenty engines, was constructed at Eastleigh Works in August 1922 and was originally numbered 748. At first the locomotives did not live up to expectations, poor steaming being a common complaint amongst enginemen. Modifications were undertaken by Maunsell which greatly improved their performance and they remained on express passenger duties until superseded by the Bulleid Pacifics. They could, however, still be seen occasionally on top link work well into the 1950s. Like many of its sister engines, *Vivien* was withdrawn in 1957, the final example of this batch surviving until March 1958. *Trevor Owen*

The pure white steam being emitted by Bulleid Pacific No.34105 *Swanage*, powering an up Bournemouth train, hangs in the freezing air near Pirbright Junction on 4th January 1959. No.34105 was a product of Brighton Works, emerging in March 1950. It was withdrawn from service in October 1964 and sent to Barry scrapyard in South Wales where it lingered intact for some years before being rescued for preservation. At the time of writing it can be seen on the Mid Hants Railway, although it is not currently operational. *Trevor Owen*

An absolutely filthy BR Standard Class 5MT 4–6–0, No.73020, heads towards London in charge of an up Bournemouth train near Pirbright Junction on 21st October 1965. At this time the Bournemouth Line was undergoing radical transformation prior to electrification, as exemplified here by the newly relaid, deep ballasted track and untidy piles of concrete troughing, in which power cables were later laid. An intensive programme of engineering works, and consequent speed restrictions, wrought havoc on the timetable during 1965/66 which resulted in a huge increase in complaints from disgruntled travellers. The train, which includes a Maunsell-designed van immediately behind the engine, comprises of a mix of Bulleid and BR Standard rolling stock. *Trevor Owen*

In another magnificent winter picture, taken on 4th January 1959, Maunsell 'King Arthur' Class No.30794 *Sir Ector de Maris* is depicted near Pirbright Junction hauling a down train. Note the second coach, which appears to be a buffet vehicle in Pullman livery. No.30794 was built as No.E794 at Eastleigh Works in March 1926 and subsequently gave almost 35 years service, being withdrawn in August 1960. *Trevor Owen*

A rather grimy Bulleid Pacific, No.34104 *Bere Alston*, makes a spirited exit from Woking with a westbound express on 6th November 1965. The tracks to Portsmouth can just be seen diverging on the extreme right of the shot, while Woking Civil Engineer's Department yard is visible behind the train. The line from London (Nine Elms) was opened as far as Woking Common station on 21st May 1838, this being the first passenger railway in Surrey. There were intermediate stations at Ditton Marsh (now Esher), Walton and Weybridge. 'Woking Common', which at the time of opening stood amidst heathland, was renamed 'Woking' in 1843, and then 'Woking Junction' two years later before reverting to 'Woking' in April 1913. Woking Common did not remain a terminus for long, because on 24th September 1838 the line was extended to Shapley Heath (now known as Winchfield), and on 10th June 1839 Basingstoke was reached. Through services from London to Southampton began on 11th May 1840. *Trevor Owen*

Viewed from the opposite side of the line to the previous picture, Bulleid Pacific No.34006 *Bude*, hauling the commuters' 5.43pm Waterloo to Salisbury train, makes a smoky departure from Woking on 17th August 1966. *Bude* has been turned out in absolutely magnificent condition, which was a hallmark of Salisbury shed at that time. Note the remarkable variety of coaches forming the train, which includes BR Standard non-gangwayed compartment stock, at least one Mk II vehicle (the second carriage behind the locomotive) plus the usual complement of familiar Bulleid coaches. Compartment coaches were only used on a small number of rush hour trains in order to increase seating capacity. Woking station, and its distinctive 1937-built power signal box, can just be discerned in the distance. *Trevor Owen*

The 12.53pm Basingstoke to Waterloo train, headed by S15 Class No.30515, speeds through West Byfleet on 25th August 1962. No.30515 was the last of a batch of twenty of these engines which was designed by Robert Urie for heavy goods traffic on the LSWR. The design was perpetuated by Maunsell, but with detail differences, the Urie-designed locomotives being immediately distinguished from the later batches by the raised running plate over the cylinders and design of the cab. West Byfleet station dates from 1st December 1887 and was originally called 'Byfleet & Woodham'. From April 1913 it was known as simply 'Byfleet', the change to its present title being made on 5th June 1950. The station initially had up and down platforms serving the (then) two track main line, but when the route was quadrupled in April 1903 the down platform became an island serving the down through and down local lines and this most unusual arrangement persists today. *Michael Allen*

Bulleid 'Merchant Navy' Pacific No.35020 *Bibby Line*, in quite presentable external condition, approaches West Byfleet at the head of the 1.22pm Waterloo to Bournemouth Central train on the same day that the previous picture was taken. Note the semaphore signalling, and goods yard on the extreme right of the photograph. No.35020 was constructed at Eastleigh Works in June 1945 and rebuilt in April 1956. It became a victim of a decision to stop heavy repairs on the class and was an early casualty, being condemned in February 1965. It is recorded as the only member of its class to have been dismantled at Eastleigh Works, this melancholy event occurring in March 1965. *Michael Allen*

Maunsell's outstanding 'Schools' Class 4–4–0s were generally more associated with the Eastern Section than the Western Section, but even so the class could be seen on the Western Section at various periods during its career. For a brief time 'Schools' class engines worked the Waterloo to Portsmouth expresses, but were displaced when this route was electrified in 1937. A number of the class was based at Bournemouth for working the lighter Waterloo expresses, until these examples were transferred to Brighton in 1946. Following the electrification of the Kent Coast lines, some 'Schools' Class engines found their way on to the Western Section in the early 1960s and could be seen on a variety of secondary passenger services such as the 12.42pm Waterloo to Basingstoke semi-fast train, seen here passing Weybridge behind No.30921 *Shrewsbury* on 25th August 1962. Unfortunately, all of the surviving members of this celebrated class were withdrawn from traffic *en masse* at the end of that year although three have been preserved. Note the electric unit in the Chertsey line up bay platform. *Michael Allen*

In the 1930s there was substantial residential development along the main line from Waterloo and house builders offered financial contributions to the Southern Railway in the hope that they might be persuaded to provide new stations for London commuters. Sometimes the railway authorities obliged, and put a considerable effort into erecting a station of which the local community could feel proud, Byfleet & New Haw being such an example. Perhaps this apparent extravagance depended on the size of the inducement being offered by the builder or the railway's own estimate of the potential! Hersham station, between Walton-on-Thames and Esher, was not so lucky, the main structure being a steel-framed timber building. The station was awkwardly sited on an embankment, the platforms being reached by wooden stairs under a corrugated asbestos roof. No subway or footbridge was provided. In this view of Hersham station, Bulleid Pacific No.34002 *Salisbury* is depicted passing through, apparently at the head of the 10.54am Waterloo to Basingstoke train sometime in the mid-1960s. No.34002, the oldest unmodified member of its class at that time, was expected to be set aside for preservation in the National Collection, but the choice was changed to No.34051 *Winston Churchill* after the latter engine hauled Sir Winston's funeral train in January 1965. *J. Spencer Gilks*

When the line from London (Nine Elms) to Woking Common opened for business on 21st May 1838, an intermediate station was built at Ditton Marsh, which today is known as Esher. The station underwent several changes of name, and from 1844 until 1913 was known as 'Esher & Claremont', before its name was abbreviated to 'Esher'. From 1934 to 1955 the station was called 'Esher for Sandown Park', before reverting to 'Esher' once more. The rebuilding of Esher station with four tracks was completed in April 1888, and the new facilities included royal waiting rooms for the Duchess of Albany, Queen Victoria's daughter-in-law, who lived at Claremont. Here, the down 'Bournemouth Belle' is seen speeding through Esher on a sunny day in August 1962. Motive power is provided by 'Merchant Navy' Pacific No.35020 *Bibby Line* which, by sheer chance, is also depicted in a previous picture. *Geoff Rixon*

On the bright afternoon of 11th March 1967, Bulleid Pacific No.34093 *Saunton* is seen hauling an up express through New Malden, towards the end of its journey to London. Mercifully, not quite all SR locomotives were encrusted with grime during the dying days of steam, and No.34093 appears to be in reasonable external condition. The train is made up of an assortment of BR Standard and Bulleid coaching stock, which was normal practice on the Southern Region at that time. *David Clark*

READING TO REDHILL

The Reading to Redhill line was opened throughout by the Reading, Guildford and Reigate Railway in 1849, but the various sections had different opening dates. The stretches of route between Reading and Farnborough plus Redhill and Dorking both opened for business on 4th July. Extensions of these two sections, to Ash Junction and Shalford Junction respectively were brought into use on 20th August, on which date the LSWR's line from Alton to Guildford, via Ash, was also commissioned thus permitting through working between Reading and Guildford. Through working between Reading and Redhill began on 15th October 1849 when the LSWR's Guildford to Godalming section of the Portsmouth Line was opened, thus closing the short, last remaining gap between Guildford and Shalford Junction. Apart from the section owned by the LSWR, the line was acquired by the South Eastern Railway in March 1852. In this picture, taken at North Camp station on 21st September 1962, a Maunsell U Class 'Mogul', No.31631, is seen leaving with a train bound for Guildford. North Camp station, opened in 1858 to serve some of the army bases around Aldershot, was officially known at one time as 'North Camp & Ash Vale for South Farnborough', quite an impressive title for such a modest station! *Alan Jarvis*

Class T9 4–4–0 No.30724 was photographed on a Reading to Guildford train near Ash on 13th March 1959. The train comprises a set of three BR Standard coaches in carmine and cream livery, plus a couple of vans. The T9s, introduced by Dugald Drummond in 1899, were one of the most attractive pre-grouping designs and this example was one of 51 machines built by Dubs & Co of Glasgow. A further batch of 15 locomotives was built at Nine Elms with slight variations from the earlier engines including wider cabs and driving wheel splashers. In the 1920s the T9s, which were known to enginemen as 'Greyhounds' were rebuilt by Urie with superheaters and extended smokeboxes, modifications which further improved the free running characteristics of these engines. The class ended its days in the West Country in 1961, apart from No.30120 which was earmarked for preservation as part of the National Collection and ran in ordinary service as LSWR No.120 for a further two years. *Trevor Owen*

Another Class T9-hauled Reading to Guildford train is seen in this picture, which was taken at Ash Junction on a sunny 10th March 1956. On this occasion the engine was No.30719, which came from the same batch as No.30724 (seen in the previous shot). By this time the line to Tongham, on the left of the photograph, had long since lost its passenger trains, and had been reduced to a 'long siding' serving a gas works at Aldershot. Note that this section of the Reading to Redhill line was electrified between Ash and Guildford when electric trains were introduced between Aldershot and Guildford in 1939. *Trevor Owen*

Trains leaving Guildford towards Reading are faced with a taxing, tightly curved 1 in 100 climb, which starts almost at the platform end and continues for two miles. Nearly all Reading-bound trains stopped at Guildford, so this must have presented quite a challenge for enginemen working a heavy freight or summer holiday train, particularly from a standing start. Fortunately, most ordinary passenger workings along the route consisted of only three or four coaches, so usually the steep ascent did not cause locomotive crews too many problems. Here, GWR-designed 4300 Class 2–6–0 No.6385 is seen making an apparently effortless climb away from Guildford with the 4.40pm Redhill to Reading Southern train on 25th August 1962. *Michael Allen*

A pair of filthy Bulleid Q1 Class 0-6-0s, Nos 33015 and 33009, hauling a Civil Engineer's Dept. working, wait for the road at Guildford on 4th October 1964. The first railway to reach the town was a branch from Woking Junction (later simply Woking) which opened on 5th May 1845. During the next 25 years the station was progressively enlarged in piecemeal fashion, which included the addition of a track with platforms on both sides, which was quite a rare feature. Despite these developments, or perhaps because of them, Guildford station remained a rather ramshackle establishment until rebuilding took place in 1887, the work including new passenger facilities and offices on the down side, together with a bay platform for trains on the Guildford New Line, which ran to Surbiton via Effingham Junction. Further works and widening of the layout occurred in 1898, but curiously the track with platforms on each side remained and caused confusion to passengers who were used to trains leaving from only one platform, and not two! In addition, trains to London sometimes departed in opposite directions, which doubtless caused further confusion to the unwary traveller. By the 1980s the station was in an extremely dilapidated condition, a disgrace to the town it served, and it must have been much to the relief of passengers when it was totally rebuilt at the end of that decade. *Roy Hobbs*

The North Downs provide a distinctive and attractive backdrop to this picture of Maunsell S15 Class 4–6–0 No.30835 ambling downhill through Gomshall & Shere station with a westbound freight on 28th April 1962. A few minutes before this shot was taken the S15 would have been doing battle with the long 1 in 96 climb out of the Mole Valley, which presented a severe test for crews of heavy goods trains. When the line through Gomshall was opened, two temporary platforms – at Gomshall, and Shere Heath – were provided to test public demand. The latter was soon deemed to be unnecessary, however, and was closed. A permanent station was constructed by the SER at Gomshall in 1852, the main building being on the up (north) side. Note the gas lamps and wooden barrows, both items of station furniture that are now very rarely seen. *Graham Hoare*

On a sunny spring day in April 1964, Maunsell S15 Class 4–6–0 No.30839 drifts down Gomshall Bank with a Redhill-bound passenger train. The picture was taken near the delightfully named Deerleap Wood, which is about two miles east of Gomshall. The bridge, which is just visible above the carriages, carries a minor road across the line. No.30839 was one of the last members of its class in active use, being among the final batch of withdrawals which occurred in September 1965. *David Clark*

Surrey's close proximity to London, and its image as the stockbrokers' county, have perhaps caused its scenic attractions to be overlooked, the area around Dorking being particularly beautiful. In this portrait of a train in the landscape, a Maunsell 'Mogul' heads towards Guildford near Ranmore Common, just west of Dorking, on 7th May 1961. The heavily wooded North Downs form an exceedingly pretty and picturesque backdrop. *Graham Hoare*

Above BR Standard 2–6–4T No.80144 enters Deepdene Station on a frosty 18th January 1964 with the 11.05am Reading Southern to Redhill train. In the mid-1960s the future of this valuable cross-country link was in doubt and, as part of their economy drive, BR demolished many of the station buildings including the brightly painted, but probably rather squalid, wooden SER structures seen here. The historic, but neglected, station building at Dorking Town (now Dorking West) was also destroyed at about the same time, leaving the two Dorking stations on this route with featureless platforms and bus stop shelters. The Reading to Redhill line was heavily used during both world wars and Dorking, in particular, played a crucial role in the Southern Railway's 1939–45 war effort. With the threat of war increasing, it purchased the Deepdene Hotel, an 1830s mansion, which was hurriedly converted to offices, the intention being that it would become their wartime headquarters. When hostilities started many departments were transferred from Waterloo and underground communications bunkers were established, thus enabling staff to control train movements on all parts of the system. Prime Minister Winston Churchill's special train took refuge at Dorking for a time. *Michael Allen*

BR Standard Class 4MT 2–6–0 No.76030 heads the 9.45am Reading to Redhill train near Buckland, between Betchworth and Reigate, on 3rd October 1964. No.76030 was not an indigenous SR locomotive and actually started its career at Stratford shed, in East London. It was later based at March in Cambridgeshire, before being displaced by diesels and moving to the SR in the early 1960s. During its stay at March it presumably worked over single track routes and was fitted with automatic single line tablet collection equipment. This was located in a recess beneath the cab windows. By the time of this picture the equipment had been removed, but the recess can just be discerned on the cab side. For many years Buckland tile works, which had a private siding, was a useful source of traffic for the railway. During the Second World War the site was converted to an ammunition and petrol storage depot, which included the installation of additional sidings. A loop was also provided on the up line and a new signal box constructed to control movements. After the cessation of hostilities the site was used for a time as a solid fuel depot. *Mike Hudson*

Opposite In this extremely rare and interesting colour picture of an LSWR Drummond-designed L12 Class 4–4–0, No.30434 is seen at the head of an eastbound train, near Deepdene. This portrait was taken in superb winter lighting conditions on Christmas Eve 1954. Twenty of these locomotives were built in 1904–05 and were later rebuilt by Urie from 1915 onwards. All of the class were still in traffic at the time of nationalisation, No.30434 being the last survivor which was withdrawn in 1955, so this picture is of considerable historical merit. *Neil Davenport*

Photographed in arctic weather conditions, the 6.50am Reading to Redhill train approaches Buckland siding behind GWR 4300 Class 2–6–0 No.6385 in February 1962. The snow-covered North Downs are visible in the background. No.6385 also appears in an earlier photograph in this section of the book, which is explained by the fact that this engine was allocated to Reading WR shed for a time. One can only admire the hardy photographer who turned out in the fairly early morning, in bitterly cold weather, to take this excellent shot. *Roy Hobbs*

A typical scene from the last years of steam working on the Reading to Redhill line when Maunsell 'Moguls' virtually monopolised passenger services. The location of this shot is clearly identified, the train being the 9.03am Reading to Redhill working with N Class 2–6–0 No.31862 in charge. At the time of this picture the days of steam-worked passenger trains were numbered, and had only three more months to run before diesel units took over. At least No.31862 remained active on the line until the end, being recorded in action on a passenger duty on the very last day of regular steam operation, which was 3rd January 1965. Much of the station and lineside equipment seen here has long since gone, but at least the signal box remains. Note the third rails for electric traction which were laid when Reigate was added to the Southern Railway's electrified network in July 1932. *Mike Hudson*

The County of Surrey was hardly renowned for its industrial locomotive fleet and one of the best known sites where industrial engines could be found was at the Dorking Lime Company's works at Betchworth. At one time three standard gauge locomotives were employed to shunt between the lime kilns and the main line. One of these was this diminutive 0–4–0T No.3 *Baxter*, which was supplied to the company by Fletcher Jennings & Co. of Whitehaven, Cumberland, in 1877 (works No.158). The engine ran without a number until about the 1920s, when the number and original name *Captain Baxter* were applied, Captain Baxter being a past chairman of the company. In 1947 its name was abbreviated to simply *Baxter*, by which it has been known ever since. The quarries at Betchworth were closed in 1959 and, as a result of the generosity of the late Major E.W. Taylerson of the Dorking Lime Co., *Baxter* subsequently found a new home at Sheffield Park on the Bluebell Railway, where this attractive and unique little engine can still be seen today. *Graham Hoare*

THE TONGHAM BRANCH

The single line from Ash Junction, on the SER Reading to Guildford section, to Farnham was opened to passenger traffic on 8th October 1849 and an intermediate station called Ash (later Ash Green) was constructed. A public freight siding was provided at Tongham and from October 1856 passenger trains stopped there to serve a new military depot which had been established in the area. A proper station was subsequently provided at Tongham. Strangely, the line beyond Tongham was doubled in 1884, just at a time when business had started to decline as a result of the opening of the Farnham–Aldershot–Ash connection in 1882. In 1926 the stations at Ash Green and Tongham were converted to unstaffed halts, and in 1930 the route was singled. Passenger services continued for a further seven years until the inevitable withdrawal came in July 1937, and this route gained an unenviable distinction when it became the first in Surrey to lose its passenger trains. The line beyond Tongham was eventually closed completely, and lifted in 1954, while the Tongham to Ash Junction section survived as a siding, primarily to supply Aldershot Gas Works, which was served by a short branch which diverged just west of Tongham station. The works was shut in June 1960, leaving occasional movements of sugar beet as the only traffic and even those ceased at the end of the same year. In this view, Bulleid Q1 Class 0–6–0 No.33025 is seen marshalling a train of sugar beet in late 1960.
J. Spencer Gilks

THE PORTSMOUTH DIRECT LINE

Until the opening of the Guildford to Havant line, passengers from London to Portsmouth had the unenviable choice of travelling the longer route via Brighton or using the shorter route via Gosport which involved crossing Portsmouth Harbour on the ferry. In 1844 two schemes to provide better communication between Portsmouth and the Capital were proposed, but at first neither received parliamentary approval. During the summer of 1846 however, the 'Direct London & Portsmouth Railway', which involved a route via Epsom, Dorking, Godalming and Petersfield, received the Royal Assent and a branch from Guildford to Godalming – which was part of another proposal put forward by a different company – was also sanctioned. The former scheme failed due to lack of finance, but at least the branch to Godalming was built, opening in October 1849. The citizens of Portsmouth were frustrated by the lack of a direct route to London and this provided the incentive for a 'contractors' group', led by the celebrated railway contractor Thomas Brassey, to construct a link from Godalming to Havant. The single line was sanctioned in 1853 and regular services commenced in 1859. The cheaply built route largely followed the lie of the land, and suffered from many tight curves and severe gradients. The line was converted to double track in 1878. The route was electrified in 1937 and since that time steam traction has hardly had a prominent role, being mostly confined to goods workings. During the mid-1960s, however, the Portsmouth Direct Line was used at weekends by Waterloo to Bournemouth (and vice versa) trains diverted due to engineering works on the main line. It is a pity that, apart from diverted trains, there was so little steam activity along the route which ran through some picturesque scenery and had, as previously stated, very fierce gradients, ideal conditions for steam photographers. For example, on the section in Surrey, apart from a short dip just south of Witley, the line climbed all of the way from Guildford to a summit just before Haslemere, the final four miles being graded at 1 in 80. Here, Bulleid Pacific No.34004 *Yeovil*, hauling a diverted Waterloo to Southampton Docks boat train, is seen passing Haslemere on 19th September 1965. *Mike Hudson*

Another scene at Haslemere, showing a very grimy Bulleid Pacific, No.34034 *Honiton*, heading north with a Waterloo-bound train on 10th October 1965. Haslemere station is just visible towards the end of the train. *David Wigley*

The Bulleid Pacifics were renowned for their power and particularly excellent performance when climbing heavy gradients. In this shot, No.34104 *Bere Alston* is depicted climbing the 1 in 80 gradient near Haslemere with a diverted Waterloo to Bournemouth express on a sunny 10th October 1965. After twelve miles of almost continuous climbing from Guildford, the Pacific appears to be 'blowing off', thus providing ample testament to the magnificent free steaming abilities of the boiler, though it must be admitted that the load in this case is only a modest eight coaches. Note the attractive location of this picture, with woodland stretching in all directions as far as the eye can see.
David Wigley

BR Standard Class 5MT 4–6–0 No.73171 exerts maximum effort as it climbs the unrelenting 1 in 80 gradient from Witley to Haslemere with a diverted express in March 1966. The location is near the hamlet of Stroud, about three miles north of Haslemere. Despite appearing here to be in fine fettle, No.73171 had only a little over six months of life remaining after this shot was taken, being withdrawn from traffic in October 1966. At that time, the run down of the SR steam fleet was proceeding apace and modern engines with trivial defects would often be condemned. *Roy Hobbs*

The dearth of steam traction on scheduled services over the Portsmouth Direct Line meant that it was an extremely popular route for railtours, and here one of these trains is seen at the same location as the previous picture, with No.34052 *Lord Dowding* in charge. The train was a Southern Counties Touring Society special, which started at London Bridge behind a BR Standard 2–6–4T locomotive and visited the Merton Park branch before No.34052 took over for the run from Wimbledon to Salisbury via Epsom, Guildford and Eastleigh. The participants then visited the Ludgershall branch before returning to London Victoria via Basingstoke, Reading and Redhill behind a 'Merchant Navy' Pacific …

… with the smoke from No.34052 billowing back along the train, the special seen in the previous view creates a stirring image as it passes the photographer. *Lord Dowding* still has a lot of climbing ahead before Haslemere is reached. Note the two enthusiasts leaning out of the window and doubtless listening to the distinctive three-cylinder exhaust beat being produced by the locomotive.
Both photos David Clark

The Portsmouth Direct Line was, as previously mentioned, constructed very cheaply, with many tight curves and some very demanding gradients. The sinuous and hilly nature of the route is exemplified in this illustration of an enthusiasts' special working approaching Witley on 18th June 1967, just a few weeks before the end of SR steam. The train is climbing on a gradient of 1 in 82 and negotiating a sharp bend at the same time! This train was the last privately sponsored tour to run on the Southern Region prior to the cessation of steam traction. Motive power was provided by BR Standard Class 5MT No.73029, in green livery, and unrebuilt Bulleid Pacific No.34023 *Blackmore Vale*. The latter engine can still be seen today on the Bluebell Railway in Sussex. The highlight of the day for the participants was a steam-hauled journey along the Swanage branch. *David Clark*

THE GUILDFORD TO HORSHAM LINE

Surrey is unique among English counties because it retains almost all of its original railway network, the only line that succumbed during the wave of closures in the Beeching era being the branch from Guildford to Horsham. The Horsham & Guildford Direct Railway opened on 2nd October 1865 with stations in Surrey at Bramley, Cranleigh and Baynards. The LBSCR contributed to the cost of construction and purchased the promoting company in 1864. Baynards station had a passing loop from the outset, while Bramley gained similar provision in 1876. Strangely, Cranleigh, which was the largest intermediate settlement on the line by far, had to wait until 1880 until it was similarly enlarged. Regular passenger services consisted at first of a mere four trains each way on weekdays which was in later years augmented to eight, with four trains on Sundays. The LBSCR was sometimes accused by Cranleigh residents of making good connections with its own services at Horsham, at the expense of providing proper connections with LSWR trains at Guildford, which offered much shorter journey times to London. The train service was always unenterprising, being slow and infrequent, and despite considerable population growth at Cranleigh little was done to attract passengers, so it was not surprising that the government agreed to closure, which occurred in June 1965, just four months before the line would have reached its centenary. In the early 1960s a mixture of pre-grouping tank locomotives could be seen at work on the line including, for a brief period, interlopers in the shape of SECR H Class 0–4–4Ts. Latterly, LMSR-designed Ivatt 2–6–2Ts were the staple motive power and here No.41299 is seen ambling along between Bramley & Wonersh and Cranleigh with the 1.34pm *ex*-Guildford on 27th June 1964. *Michael Allen*

A charming everyday scene at Cranleigh, with a local postman waiting patiently on the platform to load mail on to the approaching Guildford-bound train, which is hauled by an unidentified Ivatt 2–6–2T locomotive running bunker first. This photograph was taken on 10th April 1965, just over two months before the line was closed. *David Wigley*

On 12th June 1965, the very last day of scheduled passenger services on the branch, the 6pm Horsham to Guildford train – hauled by LMSR Ivatt 2–6–2T No.41287 – enters Cranleigh station, watched by spectators on the platforms and apparently accompanied by exploding detonators on the track. This train, and the 7.34pm Guildford to Horsham return, were especially augmented to six coaches for 'last day' mourners and were probably the heaviest scheduled trains seen on the line for many years. Mercifully, this line remains the only one in Surrey to have closed in BR days, so this was a unique event in the county. *Trevor Owen*

This view of Cranleigh, taken on 18th June 1960, depicts the 3.09pm Horsham to Guildford, with LSWR M7 Class 0–4–4T No.30051 in charge, apparently waiting to cross an up train. The enginemen can be seen on the extreme right sitting on the platform seat. The M7s were introduced to the line in Southern Railway days and became a familiar sight on the route until the early 1960s. Cranleigh benefited considerably from the arrival of the railway, which assisted the transformation of the village into a residential settlement. In 1861 its population was 1,363, but during the following forty years it more than doubled. Until June 1867 Cranleigh had been known as 'Cranley', the name being changed at the request of the Post Office which had apparently been experiencing confusion with Crawley. *Michael Allen*

The Guildford to Horsham line was constructed under the auspices of the LBSCR so trains towards Horsham were known as up workings and those in the opposite direction were down trains. Presumably Guildford-bound trains suddenly became up workings when they reached Peasmarsh Junction, where the line from Horsham joined the Portsmouth Direct Line! Here an unidentified three-coach up train from Guildford to Horsham enters Cranleigh station behind Bulleid Q1 Class 0–6–0 No.33012 on 10th October 1964. Q1s regularly worked passenger trains over the line from the late 1950s, and during the summer months they could be seen powering lengthy Sunday seaside excursions from Reading, and other centres in the Thames Valley, to Brighton. They worked as far as Horsham, where another engine would take over for the rest of the run to the coast. Unfortunately, these trains ceased in 1962 when the line was closed on Sundays for the first time, although Q1 Class locomotives continued to appear on other, much less arduous, passenger duties as seen here, plus goods workings. *David Wigley*

In this melancholy view of Baynards station taken on 10th April 1965, just two months before closure, the tracks in the goods yard are already being lifted. LMSR Ivatt Class 2MT 2–6–2T No.41294, hauling a set of three Bulleid coaches, is seen departing to Guildford. There was a chemical works at Baynards which was served by a private siding located just north of the station. When freight workings were withdrawn in September 1962 the connection into the works was reportedly severed, but had to be hastily reinstated when it was discovered that traffic to the works, mostly wagons of sulphur, was to continue. These workings continued right up to closure. *David Wigley*

An October 1963 view of the pretty Baynards station with Ivatt 2–6–2T No.41287 waiting at the head of a Horsham-bound train. Baynards was famous for its superb displays of dahlias, some of which are visible in this view. The flowers attracted many visitors, but sadly the vast majority of them arrived by car. Baynards station was built to appease Lord Thurlow, who owned Baynards Park, whose land the line's promoters wanted to cross. The railway company obtained the land at a favourable price, and in return constructed the station to serve the estate. Baynards station's quiet location and idyllic setting ensured that it was often in demand from film companies. It was used for this purpose as long ago as 1941, but perhaps the best known work filmed on the line was BBC Television's *The Railway Children* in 1957. This series made extensive use of the railway and the sequences involved LSWR T9 Class 4–4–0 No.30310, which was quite a stranger on the line. Subsequently, Baynards was used for around half a dozen further films. *David Wigley*

WEST CROYDON TO WIMBLEDON

The county of Surrey has little heavy industry, so it is, perhaps, difficult to believe that this shot of an industrial area was actually taken in the county. The location is Waddon Marsh, on the West Croydon to Wimbledon line, and the train, hauled by W Class 2–6–4T No.31919, is the 10.30am coal empties from Croydon 'B' power station to Norwood yard, which was photographed from the Purley Way roadbridge in April 1961. Part of the power station is just visible on the left of the picture. The train is about to join the electrified single track 'main line' and will then cross over onto the goods only line which can be seen on the extreme right of the picture. The spur immediately to the left of the engine ran round the back of Waddon Marsh Halt (behind the photographer on the other side of Purley Way), and connected into the extensive site of Croydon gas works, which had its own internal system worked by industrial engines. Other rail-connected premises in the area included a British Road Services depot, which generated considerable parcels traffic; the canopy of its loading dock is just visible immediately above the locomotive's smoke. In addition, there was a variety of other factories in the vicinity, including a foundry, paper processing plant and a depository for the Science Museum, all of which boasted a rail connection. *Paul Leavens*

The route from West Croydon to Dorking was electrified in stages in the 1920s, while the section on to Horsham was similarly modernised in 1938. From that time steam workings were largely restricted to freight trains and, perhaps, the occasional seaside excursion train. Consequently, colour pictures of steam trains on this route are extremely rare and largely confined to shots of railtours. Here, a Victoria to Cranleigh ramblers' special is depicted entering West Croydon behind Maunsell Q Class 0–6–0 No.30549 in June 1961. Note the elevated signal box above the first coach of train. This section of line was part of the London & Croydon Railway which opened from London Bridge to West Croydon on 1st June 1839. The route southwards from Croydon to Epsom opened on 10th May 1847. West Croydon has always been very much the poor relation of the two principal Croydon stations, and has never enjoyed main line status, unlike its neighbour, East Croydon, which is much the busier of the two. *Colin Hogg*

WEST CROYDON TO DORKING AND HORSHAM

The same locomotive is seen again, this time at Epsom on 8th June 1958, heading the 'West Sussex Downsman' railtour from London to Midhurst. Note the splendid signal gantry which has, alas, long since been removed in favour of colour light signals. No.30549 was built at Eastleigh Works in September 1939, the final member of a class of twenty locomotives to be constructed. In 1955 the engine was fitted with a BR Class 4 plain blastpipe and an ugly stovepipe chimney, as a result of draughting and steaming trials carried out at Swindon Works. In July 1963 No.30549 became the first of its class to be condemned. Sister engine No.30541 was saved for preservation and at the time of writing can be seen on the Bluebell Railway. *Neil Davenport*

On a sunny morning in July 1963, Bulleid Pacific No.34012 *Launceston* is seen leaving Dorking North with the 5.13am London Bridge to Brighton via Steyning train. This was principally a 'mails, parcels and newspaper' train which also conveyed passenger traffic, but it is unlikely that such an early morning working was heavily patronised, apart from night shift workers. In addition to serving a number of minor stations in the London suburban area which were probably not served by any other steam trains, it also formed the first down train of the day along the Steyning line, so the 5.13am was quite an interesting working. Its ancestry can be traced back at least to before the First World War, when it left London Bridge at the later time of 5.30am. The 5.13am disappeared from the timetable at the end of the 1963 summer service and was partly replaced by the 7.19am Horsham to Brighton train, so at least Steyning line passengers were still catered for. *Roy Hobbs*

The date of 13th June 1965 will be long remembered by railway enthusiasts in the south of England, because the highly scenic Eridge to Hailsham 'Cuckoo' line and Horsham to Guildford branch both closed to passengers on that date. These sad events were commemorated by the Locomotive Club of Great Britain's 'Wealdsman' railtour which included in its itinerary the Dorking to Horsham line which, by that time, was totally bereft of steam traction. That was a pity, because the line traverses some pleasant countryside and is heavily graded. Here, No.34050 *Royal Observer Corps* climbs the 1 in 100 gradient between Dorking North and Holmwood on the first leg of the tour. *Roy Hobbs*

THE EPSOM DOWNS BRANCH

Above Completed in May 1865, the four miles long branch from Sutton to Epsom Downs was primarily built to handle race traffic. It was promoted by the Banstead & Epsom Downs Railway Company, which was purchased by the LBSCR in 1864. Apart from on race days, passenger traffic was extremely light, and for many years trains did not venture beyond Banstead after the early evening. The fortunes of the line were transformed by electrification which occurred on 17th June 1928, and considerable housing development took place along the length of the branch. It is unlikely that many pictures of scheduled steam freight workings on the branch were taken, so the illustrations in this section are confined to railtours. Here, rebuilt Bulleid Pacific No.34089 *602 Squadron* stands at Epsom Downs station after arrival with a Southern Counties Touring Society railtour on 5th June 1966. There was an extensive site here, consisting of nine platforms, primarily designed to accommodate race trains, but concentration of this traffic on the more conveniently sited Tattenham Corner station made these facilities largely redundant. In the late 1980s almost all of the railway property was sold off for development, part of the deal being that the developer would provide a new, but much more modest, terminal station. *Neil Davenport*

Facing page On 5th July 1964 the Locomotive Club of Great Britain sponsored a railtour of various SR lines in Surrey and South London. Titled the 'Surrey Wanderer', the train included the Epsom Downs, Caterham and Tattenham Corner branches in its itinerary, routes where the sight of a steam hauled passenger train was exceedingly unusual. Despite the fact that many suitable 'Southern' engines were still available at that time, the LCGB selected BR Standard Class 2MT 2–6–0 No.78038 to haul the train, undoubtedly a rare class south of the River Thames – perhaps that was the attraction! The Class 2MT was specially commandeered from Willesden shed, where it was based. LSWR Class M7 0–4–4T No.30053 was also employed for some sections of the tour. Here, No.78038 is seen at the unlikely location of Banstead Downs, on the outward journey along the Epsom Downs branch. *Roy Hobbs*

Passing a delightful lower quadrant signal, No.78038 approaches Banstead station with the return working of the train seen in the previous shot. *Roy Hobbs*

THE TATTENHAM CORNER BRANCH

The Tattenham Corner Branch was proposed by independent entrepreneurs who wished to promote residential development in the Chipstead Valley, and who also sought a share of the race traffic to the Epsom racecourse. They obtained the necessary parliamentary powers, and the South Eastern Railway agreed to work the new line before absorbing the promoting companies in 1899. The first section to be opened, on 2nd November 1897, was the single-track stretch from Purley to Kingswood and Burgh Heath. This was extended westwards to Tadworth and Walton-on-the-Hill on 1st July 1900. Doubling was completed by November 1900. The last section to the terminus at Tattenham Corner, which was immediately adjacent to the racecourse, was commissioned on 4th June 1901. Some of the line's stations were quite ornate, particularly Kingswood where the residence of the line's principal promoter was situated. From 1902 until 1928, when the branch was electrified, traffic to Tattenham Corner was restricted to race trains and occasional summer excursions with daily services terminating at Tadworth. The line passes through some picturesque countryside, as exemplified in this shot of an unidentified LBSCR K Class 'Mogul' heading up the Chipstead Valley towards Tattenham Corner on a short freight train in May 1962, shortly before such workings came to an end. *Roy Hobbs*

Above In this tranquil rural scene, the LCGB's 'Surrey Wanderer' railtour, hauled by LSWR M7 Class No.30053, heads up the Chipstead Valley, between Chipstead and Kingswood stations, on 5th July 1964. The M7 locomotive is worthy of mention, because it had been withdrawn from service in May 1964, to be followed the following month by all the remaining examples of the class which had been retained at Bournemouth for duties on the Lymington branch. It was presumably temporarily reinstated to traffic to work this tour. It has henceforth led a most eventful life. In 1967 it was shipped to America for preservation at a museum in Vermont, and remained across the Atlantic until rescued by the 'Southern Repatriation Group' in 1987. At the time of writing it can be seen hauling trains on the delightful Swanage Railway in Dorset. *Roy Hobbs*

Facing page, top Not long before this picture was taken at Tattenham Corner in June 1962 the platform would have been thronged with racecourse officials, local dignitaries, railway managers and a bevy of security men, as HM the Queen and HRH the Duke of Edinburgh stepped from the Royal Train after their traditional journey from Victoria. Hopefully, the arrangements went according to plan on this occasion and everybody could relax once the Royal party had departed for the racecourse. A couple of locomotive inspectors are chatting to the crew of immaculate Maunsell 'Schools' Class 4–4–0 No.30926 *Repton* as it simmers in the platform before returning to Stewarts Lane depot with the empty stock. HM the Queen normally returned to London by road. This was the last year that a member of this class worked the Royal Train, because all the surviving 'Schools' Class engines were withdrawn from traffic at the end of the year, and indeed steam haulage of this prestigious working ceased altogether after 1964. The layout at Tattenham Corner was extremely generous, with six 20ft wide gravelled platforms which varied in length from 550 to 750 ft. Operation in the days of steam was simplified by the provision of engine release roads between each pair of platform lines. On the western side there was a dock available for the handling of horseboxes, and there were brick-built stables for the use of the horse owners and their staff. The station building was a modest, wooden-framed, slate-roofed structure with typical SER weather boarding. It was intended to be a temporary measure until something finer could be built, but in the event it lasted almost a hundred years until it was demolished during a serious shunting mishap in 1993. A most unusual feature was a raised lawn created by surplus spoil from levelling the station site. This was known locally as 'The Mound' and provided railway officials with a grandstand view of the finishing straight. *Roy Hobbs*

Left At its zenith in the 1920s, the layout at Tattenham Corner was substantial, and could hold in its platforms and sidings the sizeable total of 24 full length trains. A 54ft locomotive turntable was provided on the eastern side of the site. The decline in both race and horsebox traffic led to the abandonment of much of the facilities, and by 1970 only three platform faces plus an electrified siding remained. A particularly interesting feature of operations on race days was the use of steam locomotives with Westinghouse brake equipment, to shunt electric stock onto non-electrified sidings, or 'off the juice' in railwaymen's parlance. In this view LBSCR K Class 'Mogul' No.32345 (which was fitted with air brakes) is seen apparently performing such duties on Derby Day 1954. Note that the 4-SUB electric unit on the adjacent line appears to be berthed on a non-electrified siding.
Neil Davenport

EAST CROYDON TO REDHILL AND THREE BRIDGES

Bulleid Pacific No.34101 *Hartland* makes a fine sight in the evening sun as it approaches East Croydon with the lengthy 6.10pm Victoria to Brighton train via Oxted, Uckfield and Lewes in June 1961. These machines only started to be used regularly on the Oxted Line after being made redundant on the South Eastern Section by electrification, but at the time of this picture No.34101 was one of four Bulleid Pacifics still maintained by Bricklayers Arms shed for Central Section duties. *Hartland* was transferred to Brighton shed in June 1962 when Bricklayers Arms closed. The summer of that year saw the widespread introduction of diesel units on Oxted Line diagrams and, as a result, the number of steam workings saw a corresponding reduction, so it is likely that No.34101's association with the Oxted Line was very short lived. *Paul Leavens*

Photographed on a dull and damp day in March 1962, LMSR Fairburn-designed 2–6–4T No.42118 rests at East Croydon station apparently after arrival with an inter-regional freight working from Willesden. The train was photographed on the middle road between Platform Two (on the left) and Platform Three. Almost needless to say, the middle road disappeared many years ago, and the station buildings in view have also gone following extensive rebuilding in the mid-1990s. The platform awnings were also refurbished at the same time, but some of the superstructure, such as the original stanchions, was retained, so some traces of the old station will remain for many years to come. At the time of the photograph, Platform Two was used solely by down trains, including suburban services to Coulsdon North, while the other platform served as an up relief road, mainly for main line trains. No.42118 was one of a large number of 2–6–4Ts built at Derby and this particular example first saw the light of day in August 1949. When this picture was taken it was based at Willesden shed and survived in traffic there until September 1965, when that depot was closed. *Michael Allen*

The 1.46pm empty stock working from Tattenham Corner to Stewarts Lane Depot (to quote the train's official description) approaches East Croydon station behind 'Schools' Class 4–4–0 No.30926 *Repton* in June 1961. The track furthest away from the camera was reversible, and generally used as an up line for Oxted Line trains during the morning peak, while in the evening rush hour it was used for down trains, especially those on the Oxted Line. The tall trees border an attractive municipal park, an area of peace and tranquillity in central Croydon. *Paul Leavens*

The visit of the elegant Caledonian Railway 'Single' locomotive No.123, which was built by Neilson & Co. of Glasgow in 1886, was one of the highlights in the more recent history of the Brighton Line. On 15th September 1963 No.123 and LSWR T9 Class 4–4–0 No.120 hauled a Victoria to Sheffield Park railtour (via Ardingly) which is seen pausing at East Croydon. The pair worked the train as far as Haywards Heath, from where they proceeded to Brighton for servicing. During the run along the Brighton Line the T9 undoubtedly provided most of the pulling power, but later in the day No.123 proved it had plenty of a different kind of 'pulling power' when it attracted more than 2,000 admirers to Horsted Keynes! Since this picture as taken, the T9 Class engine, which is preserved as part of the National Collection, has led something of a nomadic existence and has been resident at various times on the Mid Hants and Swanage Railways. At the time of writing it can be found at Sheffield Park, on the Bluebell Railway, though it is not currently in use.
Geoff Rixon

'Southern Railway' proclaims the sign above the entrance to East Croydon station, while another sign attempts to woo passengers with a 'Frequent Electric Trains – Cheap Tickets Daily' slogan. It is difficult to believe that this picture was taken on Derby Day 1960! Surprisingly, the Southern Region's re-signing department did not have East Croydon very high on its priorities, despite it being one of the busiest stations on the region. The view seen here has since changed beyond recognition. All the old buildings have gone, and even the track layout is very different today following remodelling in the early 1980s. The old bridge is still *in situ*, but is now mostly hidden by a new bridge constructed alongside during road widening in the 1960s. The projections in the grass on the right of the picture next to the retaining wall, appear to be the remains of overhead a.c. electrification girders. The Royal Train to Tattenham Corner, hauled by 'Schools' Class No.30938 *St Olave's* is almost of secondary importance in this illustration. One wonders whether any of the passengers on the Victoria to Coulsdon North electric train, rattling along on the adjacent down local line, obtained a good view of the Royal party as they journeyed in their somewhat superior accommodation!
The late Derek Cross

Photographed on the sunny evening of 31st May 1962, the 5.25pm London Bridge to Reading/Tonbridge train is seen approaching Purley Oaks station, which serves a leafy and prosperous residential area south of Croydon. Motive power is provided by Maunsell 'Schools' 4–4–0 No.30915 *Brighton* which, in common with all its remaining sister engines, was withdrawn at the end of that year. The 'Schools' were extremely compact and competent engines, arguably Maunsell's most successful design, and the class was particularly associated with the Hastings Line for which they were designed and where they performed admirably, until diesels took over in the late 1950s. *Colin Hogg*

A railtour from London Bridge to Brighton and Seaford approaches Merstham station on 7th October 1962 with Maunsell 'Schools' 4–4–0 No.30925 *Cheltenham* in charge. This is another location that has suffered drastic changes since the end of steam. The railway now crosses the eight-lane M25 motorway on a bridge here, so nowadays it is not possible to take a picture at this spot without considerable risk to life and limb. One can only sympathise with the householders of the nearby properties who now have to tolerate the incessant roar of fast-moving traffic in the name of 'progress'. *Roy Hobbs*

A May 1963 view taken on a sunny morning at the north end of Redhill station, showing GWR-designed 'Manor' 4–6–0 No.7813 *Freshford Manor* shunting rolling stock, in this case a Southern Railway Bulleid 3-set, after arrival with the 6.50am from Reading South. Another steam-hauled train in the up main platform appears to have a bunker-first BR Standard 2–6–4T at its head. The section of line from Croydon Junction (later Norwood Junction) to Haywards Heath was opened on 12th July 1841, the stretch as far as Redhill also being used by the South Eastern Railway's trains from London to the Channel ports until the Sevenoaks cut-off was inaugurated in 1868. Redhill – an important cross-country junction – was famous for many years for the huge amounts of Royal Mail traffic, and associated van trains, which were handled at the station. On occasions the many barrowloads of mail on the platforms presented a considerable obstacle to passengers. Redhill's importance for mail traffic declined considerably following the commissioning of the Post Office's new distribution centre at Wembley in the mid-1990s. *Roy Hobbs*

A superb and fascinating bird's-eye view of the layout immediately south of Redhill station, showing (from top to bottom) the Guildford line curving away on an embankment in the middle background, the Brighton Line (immediately in front of the row of wagons) and the Tonbridge route in the foreground. The picture was taken on 17th July 1964. The rooftops of the town form the background, with the slopes of the tree-covered North Downs on the distant horizon. There are sand quarries in the Redhill area and much of this traffic was transported by rail in hopper wagons which sometimes had ill-fitting doors, thus allowing some of the contents to escape onto the track. The sidings in the foreground appear to have been used by sand wagons, judging by the liberal covering on the track! Examination of the locomotives on shed will reveal two visitors in addition to Redhill shed's usual complement of BR Standard Class 4MT 2–6–4Ts and Maunsell 'Moguls'. The GWR-designed engine is a 'Manor' 4–6–0 which had almost certainly powered the 6.50am from Reading earlier that day, that train being a regular turn for a 'Manor' at the time. The LMSR 'Black Five' is No.44951, which had failed at Haywards Heath on 8th July while taking a Newhaven to Glasgow car-sleeper train, and had been sent to Redhill for repair. It eventually left on the day this picture was taken hauling an empty pigeon van working bound for Newcastle, hence it is in steam on shed waiting to set out on the first stage of its journey home to Mirfield shed, near Leeds. *Roy Hobbs*

Above The year 1964 was the last for regular steam-hauled inter-regional excursion trains which had been such a feature of weekends on the Brighton Line. In times past some highly unusual locomotives appeared on these trains, including an LMSR 4F 0–6–0 which worked an extra from Luton in 1958, and various 'Jubilee' 4–6–0s, which ventured down to the coast on a few occasions despite being officially banned. Most of the latter were immediately impounded on arrival and returned to the LMR under special arrangements. These sorties were very much the exception however, and LMSR Class 5MT 4–6–0s were usually rostered for the excursions. On 5th June 1964 a return Dalston Junction to Hastings special, hauled by No.45379, is seen approaching Earlswood, with the fireman no doubt working hard to maintain boiler pressure on the long climb, mostly at 1 in 200 or thereabouts, from Horley to Star Lane, just beyond the Quarry Tunnel. Note the LMSR-designed rolling stock. *Mike Hudson*

Facing page, top The annual royal train from Victoria to Tattenham Corner combined with 'specials' from Gatwick Airport station to Victoria for visiting heads of state, probably ensured that the Brighton Line had very much more than its fair share of VIP special workings, and the same is still probably true today. Here Bulleid Pacific No.34088 *213 Squadron* is seen approaching Salfords with a special train conveying the Indian President to London in July 1963. No.34088 had been one of the last engines of its class allocated to Stewarts Lane shed and, with that depot's closure to steam imminent at the time of this photograph, had just been moved to Brighton. It finished its career in extremely decrepit condition on the Bournemouth Line, in marked contrast to its highly polished state in this picture. *David Clark*

Facing page, bottom A stranger in Surrey! Indeed this machine, LNER K4 Class 2–6–0 No.3442 *The Great Marquess*, could be regarded as a stranger anywhere south of the West Highland line! This class of six three-cylinder locomotives was designed by Gresley and introduced in 1937, specifically to satisfy the need for a more powerful type on the West Highland line from Glasgow to Fort William and Mallaig. No.3442 (latterly BR No.61994) was built at Darlington in June 1938 and was destined to spend all its working life at Glasgow (Eastfield) and Fort William sheds, apart from a brief spell at Thornton Junction towards the end of its career. It was withdrawn from BR service at the end of 1961 and purchased for preservation by the late Viscount Garnock, who arranged for No.3442 to be overhauled and restored to LNER colours at Cowlairs Works, Glasgow. It was subsequently based at Neville Hill shed, Leeds, from where it made numerous railtour appearances, but in more recent times has been kept at Bridgnorth, on the Severn Valley Railway. Here it is seen south of Gatwick Airport, extremely close to the (then) Sussex border, on railtour duty on 12th March 1967, during the period when it was kept at Leeds. This is the only occasion known to the author that an engine of this class has visited Surrey, so this was a totally unique event. *Neil Davenport*

THE QUARRY LINE

By the end of the nineteenth century business on the railway was growing rapidly and, in order to cater for this expansion, the LBSCR intended to widen the Brighton Line to four tracks wherever possible. Redhill's status as a busy, strategic railway centre, not to mention its flat junctions, made it a potential bottleneck, so the LBSCR planned an avoiding line between Coulsdon and Earlswood. Commonly known as the 'Quarry Line', it was opened to freight traffic in November 1899 and to passenger trains from 1st April 1900. The line involved the construction of two tunnels and excavation of deep chalk cuttings, so it was an expensive operation, but at least it gave the LBSCR its own route to Brighton, which avoided the line via Redhill which it shared with the South Eastern Railway. In this shot 'Schools' Class 4–4–0 No.30923 *Bradfield* is seen in a fortunate patch of sunshine heading a Hastings to Sheffield train near Hooley on 20th August 1960. *J. Spencer Gilks*

Maunsell N Class 2–6–0 No.31823, hauling a lengthy Wolverhampton to Hastings holiday train, threads the extremely deep chalk cutting at Star Lane on 20th August 1960. Note the carmine and cream rolling stock which comprises most of the train. The considerable earthworks necessary to build the Quarry Line through the North Downs are evident in this illustration. The siding on the right was installed to provide access to Star Lane electricity sub-station when the line was electrified in the 1930s.
J. Spencer Gilks

Maunsell 'Schools' 4–4–0 No.30929 *Malvern* approaches the Quarry Tunnel with a Hastings to Wolverhampton holiday train on 25th August 1962, a beautifully clear day. Note the neatly manicured cutting sides in the foreground, in sad contrast to today when so much of the lineside is appallingly neglected. Since this picture was taken this scene has been dramatically transformed by the construction of the M25 motorway, which today slices through the middle of the picture at the end of the cutting. Merstham station, in the background, is still very much in business, but the sidings and footbridge have gone, and even the signal box has disappeared following the replacement of traditional semaphore signalling by colour lights. *J. Spencer Gilks*

One of the most interesting locomotives to visit Redhill during the BR steam era was undoubtedly LNER-designed B1 Class 4–6–0 No.61313. The B1 powered an Edinburgh to Lewes pigeon special during June 1964, but failed on Eastbourne shed with a hot box. It left Eastbourne for Redhill on 6th July, travelling at slow speed. It seems that the shed foreman took a liking to the stranger, so consequently the interloper's sojourn at Redhill lasted for some months and it was late September before repairs had been completed. The shed staff presumably wanted to give No.61313 a trial run, so on 30th September it was employed on an empty stock working to Brighton, hardly a demanding proposition. On 1st/2nd October Redhill shed put the visitor to more serious work on stopping passenger duties to Reading, where its appearance probably created quite a stir among the local train spotting fraternity. On 3rd October it was declared to be fully recovered and is pictured climbing up to Redhill tunnel on a special freight from Earlswood to Streatham Common. This was the first stage of its long, and rather belated, journey to its home shed of Canklow, near Sheffield.
David Wigley

The maroon-liveried carriages behind the engine immediately identify this train as an inter-regional working from the South Coast to the Midlands or North of England. The first vehicle with the distinctive white, oval-shaped toilet window is of LNER Thompson design. Motive power is provided by a decidedly filthy, and therefore unidentified, Maunsell 2–6–0. The location is the southern approach to Redhill tunnel, on the Quarry Line, and the date is sometime in August 1962. *Roy Hobbs*

THE CATERHAM BRANCH

In this extremely rare colour picture of steam traction on the Caterham branch, LSWR M7 Class 0–4–4T No.30053 is seen at Caterham on railtour duty on 5th July 1964. The (then) single line 4½-miles long branch was opened by the independent Caterham Valley Railway Company on 5th August 1856. The company was in a difficult position, however, because it was operating in SER territory, but connecting with main line trains at Purley station which were controlled by the SER's rival, the LBSCR. The latter was not disposed to hold main line connections, much to the annoyance of Caterham branch passengers who were badly treated by the LBSCR. In 1859 the inevitable happened and the Caterham Company was purchased by the SER. Despite its inauspicious beginnings, the Caterham line proved to be remarkably successful in promoting residential development along the Caterham valley, which was totally undeveloped until the coming of the railway. Building of large houses was under way as early as 1860 and during the ensuing forty years the valley's population soared. By the end of the nineteenth century business along the branch was sufficiently buoyant to encourage the SER to embark on a major rebuilding of the branch and its structures. The line was doubled and the rather cramped station facilities at Caterham enlarged. The premises were completely rebuilt and the one short platform was replaced by two much longer ones. Unfortunately this work involved the demolition of the original station building, designed by Richard Wittall, whose exuberant architecture characterised the branch at the time. Electrification and further development in the 1930s building boom have combined to assure the future of this short branch. *Mike Hudson*

REDHILL TO TONBRIDGE

A picture taken in sunshine with snow on the ground, the kind of unusual weather conditions railway photographers dream about! Here, BR Standard 2–6–4T No.80153 is seen descending the short 1 in 341 incline into Redhill station with a mid-morning train from Tonbridge in December 1964, a few weeks before diesel units largely displaced steam traction on this route. The line was opened in May 1842 and, as previously mentioned, was the SER's principal route to the Kent coast until the Sevenoaks cut-off was opened in 1868. Initially, the LBSCR and SER had separate stations at Redhill – hardly a convenient arrangement for passengers – but in 1844 a new station, situated on the site of the present premises, was brought into use. In 1858 the latter station was substantially reconstructed, one of its features being canopies which extended out over the adjacent track. These were supported on iron pillars located between the through and platform lines, which were a considerable hazard to railway staff. The canopies were reconstructed, and the offending pillars removed, following the death of a Pullman conductor in 1895. For many years the station was known as 'Red Hill Junction', the description 'Junction' being phased out in the 1920s. *Roy Hobbs*

On a sunny 11th March 1961, a commendably clean BR Standard tank locomotive, No.80147, is depicted near Nutfield at the head of a Redhill to Tonbridge train. Nutfield was the second intermediate passenger and freight station in Surrey to be opened on the Redhill to Tonbridge line, the first being at Godstone. *R.C. Riley*

The western portal of Bletchingley tunnel, in the background, which is situated between Nutfield and Godstone, immediately identifies the location of this shot. The train, a local working from Tonbridge to Redhill is seen coasting along this level section of track behind BR Standard 2–6–4T No.80154 on 9th June 1962. No.80154 had a considerable claim to fame as the last locomotive built at Brighton Works, and also because it powered the final train along the famous Bluebell Line prior to closure by BR in March 1958. Despite these distinctions it was not preserved, but other members of the class survive in preservation. *R.C. Riley*

Lineside flowers provide an attractive foreground to this shot of two veteran SECR 4–4–0s near Godstone on 28th May 1961. The engines were hauling a nine-coach ramblers' special from Victoria to Hawkhurst via Redhill. The leading engine is D1 Class No.31739 which was built as a D class locomotive at Ashford Works in 1902 and rebuilt in April 1927. The train engine is No.31067, an E1 class locomotive which originally saw the light of day at Ashford in April 1908 as an E Class. It was rebuilt to an E1 in February 1920. At the time of this photograph only a handful of each class remained active, and both classes became extinct at the end of 1961. *Graham Hoare*

BR Standard tank engine No.80089 brings a train from Redhill to Tonbridge into Godstone station on the morning of 2nd January 1965. Let us hope that the steam heating was working correctly on what appears to be a very cold and frosty morning! *Michael Allen*

THE OXTED LINE

The line from South Croydon to Oxted and East Grinstead was opened on 10th March 1884, and the (then) branch line from Hurst Green to Edenbridge in Kent carried its first passenger services in January 1888. The section from South Croydon to Oxted utilised the earthworks constructed in the mid-1860s by the Surrey & Sussex Junction Railway, which were later abandoned. Known as the 'Oxted Line', the South Croydon to Oxted section has considerable gradients, some as steep as 1 in 100, in both directions as it traverses the North Downs. The summit is just south of Woldingham station. Besides being one of the most steeply graded, the route also offers some of the finest scenery of any line in this book. There is no hint of the route's scenic attractions in this shot, however, which depicts BR Standard Class 4MT 2–6–4T No.80019 passing Selsdon, in the Croydon suburbs, with the 1.08pm Victoria to Tunbridge Wells West train in May 1960. Note the extremely neglected state of the station buildings. The platforms on the right were served by electric trains operating from Elmers End to Sanderstead. *Paul Leavens*

The 5.37pm train from London Bridge to East Grinstead leaves Sanderstead behind BR Standard tank engine No.80010 on the fine evening of 31st May 1962. In the early 1960s Sanderstead was an interesting spot, being served by diesel and steam hauled Oxted Line trains, and also infrequent electric services to and from Elmers End on the Eastern Section, which terminated there. The electric trains ran along the down line (hence the third rail in this shot) for a short distance before reversing into the up platform prior to returning to Elmers End. *Colin Hogg*

Between Riddlesdown and Upper Warlingham the Oxted Line is carried over Riddlesdown Quarry on an impressive viaduct, one of the route's notable engineering features. In this magnificent photograph, BR Standard Class 4MT 2–6–4T No.80137 emits a splendid smoke effect as it crosses the lofty viaduct with the heavy 4.20pm London Bridge to East Grinstead commuter train on 2nd October 1961. *Paul Leavens*

The ancient and modern figure in this scene of Oxted station on 9th May 1954, which shows BR Standard tank No.80011 posing in the down platform. This train is a rather odd combination, consisting of a vintage SECR 'Birdcage' set of coaches, in the red livery which was in vogue on the SR at that time, plus a locomotive which had been in traffic less than three years when this shot was taken. The North Downs form a distant backdrop. No.80011 was a product of Brighton Works, being outshopped in July 1951, and survived until the very end of steam on the SR in July 1967. *Neil Davenport*

During the 1950s a sizeable batch of LMSR Fairburn tank locomotives was active on the Central Section, a total of 41 having been built at Brighton Works specifically to replace the ageing LBSCR passenger tank classes which were life expired. The 'Fairburns' were powerful and extremely competent machines and performed much sterling work on the Oxted Line for a number of years, until replaced by similar and equally excellent BR Standard engines in 1960. The Fairburn locomotives were found alternative work on other regions. In this picture, also taken on 9th May 1954, a highly polished No.42090 is seen entering Oxted station from the south with a train presumably bound for Victoria. A rake of four Maunsell coaches make up the train. *Neil Davenport*

BR Standard 2–6–4T No.80139 makes a vigorous departure from Oxted with a
southbound train on a bright spring morning in May 1961. The site of the goods yard,
on the left, is now occupied by a supermarket. *David Clark*

The 1pm Tunbridge Wells West to Oxted push-pull train is hauled across Oxted viaduct by SECR H Class 0–4–4T No.31551 on 1st June 1963. The train is formed of Maunsell stock, the rear carriage being a brake vehicle fitted with a driver's cab for push-pull operation. The handsome 150-yard long viaduct consists of three main wrought-iron lattice girder spans which are supported on brick piers. The viaduct carries the line across the waters of the infant River Eden between Oxted station and the 550-yard long Limpsfield tunnel. The first of these distinctive H Class engines was built at Ashford works in 1904, No.31551 being built in January 1905. It survived in service until January 1964 and was among the last three members of this long lived class to remain active. *Michael Allen*

Hurst Green Junction is bathed in glorious evening sunshine as BR Standard Class 4MT tank locomotive No.80152 approaches with an East Grinstead to Victoria train sometime in the early 1960s. This shot was apparently taken from the verandah of Hurst Green Junction signal box, which presumably controlled the delightful, vintage lower quadrant signal which is visible towards the rear of the train. The tracks curving away to the left led to Brighton via Uckfield and Tunbridge Wells via Groombridge, but the Beeching 'axe' destroyed this once busy network of secondary routes, and only a branch line now remains as far as Uckfield. No.80152 was reportedly the last member of its class to power a passenger working on the SR when it hauled a boat train from Southampton Central to Southampton Eastern Docks on 8th July 1967, the penultimate day of steam on the Southern Region. *Gerald Daniels*

A charming view of a Tunbridge Wells West to Oxted push-pull working, or 'motor train' as these services were sometimes known, approaching Hurst Green Junction with SECR H Class tank locomotive No.31543 in charge. *Gerald Daniels*

In this most interesting and unusual photograph W Class 2–6–4T No.31920 is depicted at Lingfield in June 1963 at the head of a banana special, probably from Avonmouth. The building on the right was apparently a ripening shed for Geest bananas and still exists today, albeit in use for other purposes. Banana trains hauled by W Class locomotives were not an everyday sight on this line, so it is likely that the photographer was party to 'inside information' regarding this working. The distinctive W Class was designed by Maunsell for heavy transfer freight working between London marshalling yards and goods depots, a type of train rarely seen today. The first five engines were built at Eastleigh in 1932 while the remaining ten were constructed at Ashford in 1935/36, No.31920 being from the latter batch. They were powerful three-cylinder machines and one of their exceptional design features was the rear bogie, which was fitted with brakes to enhance the locomotives' braking capability while working unbraked (or partially fitted) freight services. The last of the class was taken out of service in 1964. *David Clark*

A general view of the extremely neat and tidy station at Lingfield with a Tunbridge Wells West to Victoria via East Grinstead train, hauled by an unidentified BR Standard 2–6–4T, waiting the 'right away'. The county of Surrey is famous as the home to some of the nation's finest racecourses, one of the best known being Lingfield Park which was opened in 1890. The course was enlarged in 1894 and during the same year the LBSCR undertook a similar exercise at Lingfield station. A new down loop was provided thus converting the easternmost platform to an island. In addition, the platforms were extended and the loading dock behind the signal box was lengthened to cater for increasing horse traffic. There was a proposal at one time to build a line into the racecourse! Even as late as the 1950s race trains ran to Lingfield station from Victoria, Cannon Street and Brighton and, despite the short journey time, some of these specials conveyed a Pullman Car. *David Wigley*